Thought Thermometer

Cassandra Sonnenschein

BookLeaf Publishing

Presentation by *BookLeaf Publishing*

Web: www.bookleafpub.com

E-mail: info@bookleafpub.com

ISBN: 9789357212892

First edition 2023

To the teachers who looked beyond grades and believed that expressing myself would amount to something substantial.

To the friends & family who listen to, encourage and support my authentic self.

To a year 6 student who shared her compulsion to diary in poetry form.

Spoilers

what would your story amount to?
if you were just to look
at all the headings on your shelves
describing you book by book

if all the chapters or potential lives
that you could live were there
would you read them all in order?
or refrain because you care
to experience it all firsthand
no hindsight to taint the trip
live each moment, soak it in
take care to never lose your grip

Limo & Eis

trawling through books
they never fully sate her
but rather the opposite
they serve to bait her

glass shattering shard by shard
as she considers whether real life should be this
hard
is the reality we've created broken
or rather those with prominent voices outspoken

she yearns to transcend
an existence encompassing just who, what, when
rather embrace herself for who she is
like an ice cream and lemonade combo that
allows itself to fizz

she tries each day this way to light up the world
while ever seeking refuge from the chaos she is
hurled

Selbstgespräch

you always write to the future you
but what about your past?
the little girl inside of you
just focused on making things last

the girl who sat and took everything in
forever wondering where to begin
to be herself amongst everyone else
without sacrificing what she holds dear

she set off on the track we call life
determined to make everything right
she stumbled and fell
only those closest could tell
needed guidance to escape from the strife

all in her head
she knew could be said
however her body would not let her settle

learning to accept the right help
express via journal not welp
she transformed from a bud to a petal

Schwämme

wo lernt man sich die Welt kennen?
'ne Klare, Bewusster Entscheidung?
oder sind wir erstmal alle Schwämme
die einfach alles ertragen

ohne zu wissen, werden unsere Aussichten
gebaut
alles das uns gesagt wurde einfach plötzlich
geglaubt
endlich mal der Punkt angekommen ist;
herauszufinden wer du wirklich bist

Zeit nehmen

the time is ours to take
before we snap and we break
the guilt it feels so real
heaviness I long not to feel

when did I decide it's my job?
to take care of and save a whole mob
boundaries I need to enforce
before a new life I can source

Spotto

I thought we were on the lookout for yellow
not merely attempting to prevent a bellow
the one that occurs in exasperation
when you discover elements of yourself are not
your own creation

I just want to build my compass
the decision-making machine that guides us
turns out that first I need to with awareness
witness
all that I am that led up to this
only then can I hope to transform
into exactly the being I was destined to be
on the winter solstice when I was born

Curious Koalas

a teacher and a leader
a cheery grin for all who meet her
a drive to support and inspire
awareness and skills they will acquire
motivated to achieve their dreams
forever bonded as one of Miss P's teams

Feather Ruffler

am I Aussie am I German?
do I ask this to deter being certain?
that for one or both I could be received as a burden
a mixture of both I proclaim to be
for only with elements of both do I feel free to be me

friendly, open and gregarious
can sometimes be seen as reckless
settled, outrageous and honest
ruffles feathers in others' bonnets

I know now different versions of home
one with roots and the other where you feel most known
where will I end up, only time will tell
the stirrings of my heart and soul, I never can quell
who says I have to choose?
neither part am I prepared to lose

Bye-lingual

gedichte auf Deutsch sind nicht besonders
einfach
mich komplett wahr ausdrücken, kann ich
dreifach
am besten wenn ich Denglisch rede
um sich selbst zu sein braucht man viele Wege;
anziehen, Musik, worüber man gerne redet
dann findet man die richtige Freunde
unter den sind Lebensziele abgehackt

I don't answer, I respond

easy as an ocean breeze
all she wanted was to please
like a tree's new twig buried in snow
under the weight she sank below
healing slowly in the dark
she learned to reignite her spark

Jacarandas

jacarandas dot the horizon that I can see
a safe place for me
a rock where I can gather my thoughts
cockatoo, kookaburra calls they taunt

occasional squeals from friday night revellers
makes me remember when we were travellers
ready to take in each new day
before we were to travel on far away

soaking in all that life had in store
rarely ceasing because we always wanted more
new ideas, people, old new surroundings
allowed us to contemplate our own boundaries

Is it...

deficiency
anxiety
a bush turkey?
what will it take 'till I really know me?
how I am, what I want, how I need to behave
figure out how to thrive and not just be brave

Dixit
Abendessen
mit die Girls zusammen sitzen?
felt like winning the lottery, ich konnte nur
Grinsen
seit dann fühl' ich mich irgendwie immer alleine
es muss mehr als diese Hannover Zeiten geben
ich muss nur einfach versuchen weiter Dinge zu
erleben

Seeking

endless scrolling
searching for a dopamine hit
colours, ideas flashing
you feel your teeth grit
information overload
you lose your concentration
buzzing in your ears returns
not again, this overstimulation
the very thing you sought to quell
thumbs opening a promising link
society's new remedy
before you're given a chance to think

Egal

I don't care, 'ist mir egal'
ist es wirklich so schlimm zu sagen?
oder einfach ne ehrliche Antwort
wann man bekommt so viele Fragen

in einer Zeit wo jeder eine Meinung erwartet
bleibt uns irgendwo noch Stille
wo wir einfach sein können
ohne Präferenzen, nur Tee mit Kamille

'Ist mir egal' könnte eine Liebessprache sein
vielleicht sind wir damit zufrieden
wenn jemand die wir lieben
uns kurz Kraft und Wahrheit liehen

Aufgenommen

Schlafanzüge, Kissenhülle
hatte früher keine richtige Bedeutung
jetzt dass ich was hinter gelassen hab'
werden die zu meine Rettung

wir sind verbunden
auch wenn sehr weit entfernt
Facetime, WhatsApp
fühlt man es sich davon ernährt

ich wünsche ich könnte näher sein
um einfach vorbei zu kommen
die Wahrheit mit Freundinnen erfahren
im Tiny Haus
in der Gerber
sofort aufgenommen

Stand Up

denk mal an der Best Case Scenario
wo die Leute dich Supporten stattdessen sagen einfach no
hab' ich einmal im Wohnzimmer mit 26 erfahren
gequatscht, gelacht, gesungen mit jeder die da waren
eine Comedy Show wollten wir zusammen gründen
lustige Geschichten und Reime haben wir erfunden

Fluffy Friends

floppy ears
waggy tail
an excited panting smile
do you think that I could stay with you
for a little while?
the cure for all the madness in the world
a happy little scratch
when they lay their paws on you
your heart they'll forever catch

Cockatoo

I thought that I could make a difference
not just learn the art of ignorance
the wind through my ears
makes me stop short my tears

so far away from home
although in the place I became full grown
I yearn that I could share it
every thought, occurrence and habit
ponder what lies in store
without insulting the core
people I hold dear
and the ones that I found here

just wanting to feel free
to be where I feel most me
my senses exalt as I draw near to the bush
I hope it will not think my scribblings are mush